Thank You

By buying this magazine, you support small business owners and small creators!

TalesOfTheGods aims to connect the metaphysical and spiritual communities.

Cover Photo - Coincidence on Unsplash.

If you would like to write in anonymously, or join our team for the next edition feel free to send a email to TalesOTheGods@gmail.com

TalesOfTheGods, September 2021

facebook.com/groups/665578877692886

Contributors

Desirée Goulden	Owner, layout design, contributor
Owen Lee Heavenhill	Photographer, Contributor
Dana Lee Beaudreau	Founding member, Contributor

The TalesOfTheGods & Practical Witchcraft magazine is a community project. Our roster of contributors is constantly shifting. Everyone who works on the magazine takes home an equal take of the income from the sales of this magazine.

We aim to bring education and entertainment to people of all levels of experience and paths. If you have a point of view that you would like to share with the world, feel free to reach out to join us. We are currently looking for people of colour to join us. Whether you are a teacher, or just interested in taking part, we have a place for you.

Have a shop or product you want to share with the world? Contact us and we will run a free full page ad for you in the next edition! We release on every day of the wheel of the year, so it's easy to follow release dates!

We understand that there may be some who may not want to support Amazon, so we have made the shift from publishing through Kindle Direct Publishing for our paper back editions to Ingram Spark. This will allow for wider distribution (Chapters, Barns & Noble, indie book shops) for those who want to support us without supporting Amazon and Jeff Bezos.

Please know that all opinions are that of the contributor and may not reflect the team in general.

Contents

About Samhain	PAGE 2
Understanding Soul Contracts	PAGE 4
Death Rituals Around The World	PAGE 6
Grief & Cookies	PAGE 10
The Misconceptions About Ouija Boards	PAGE 12
Grief	PAGE 16
For This I am Ever Thankful	PAGE 18
What Is A Death Witch?	PAGE 20
Book Of Shadows Pages	PAGE 25
Pagans & Cremation	PAGE 30
Magazine Updates	PAGE 36

 *The Underworld Oracle Deck By Desiree Goulden*

25 Full colour cards

Works with reversed cards

Works with other decks

$23.99 Cad

https://www.thegamecrafter.com/games/the-underworld-oracle-deck

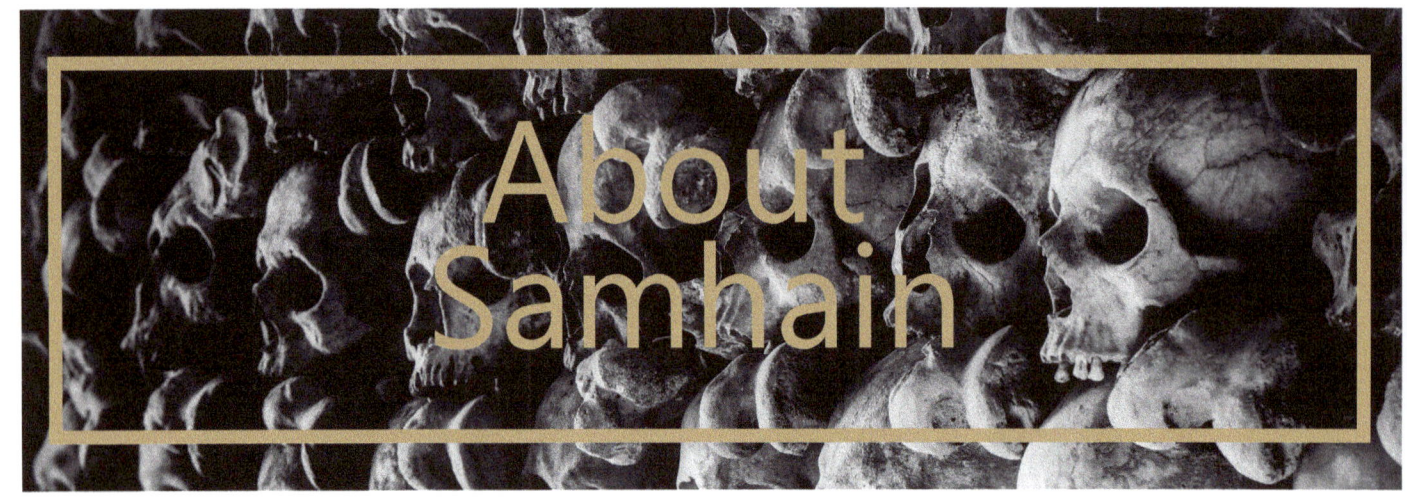

About Samhain

Samhain is the second last day on the wheel of the year. It takes from the Celtic day of the same name. Samhain is when the veil between worlds is at it's thinnest and is the time to celebrate and honor the dead. In Celtic traditions they wouldn't speak after a certain hour, held a dummy dinner for the dead, and put out carved turnips to avoid being taken as the souls of the dead are collected.

Modern Wiccan and witchy traditions in the west celebrate it on the same day as Halloween and is a little more relaxed and festive. You can dress up your altar to honor those you've lost. You can host a dummy dinner, and take part of wider cultural festivities of Halloween.

Some people regard this as the time that Persephone returns to the Underworld to reunite with Hades, so some Hellenic Pagans take this time to celebrate the two.

The colours of Samhain are: yellow, brown, and gold.

The symbols of Samhain are: mulled whine, leaves, nuts, acorns, dark loaves of bread, corn, scarecrows, scythes, and skulls.

Jim Two Snakes
Spiritual Advisor

 jimtwosnakes.net

 facebook.com/jimtwosnakes

 instagram.com/jimtwosnakes

 patreon.com/spiritualdad

Many people think the term Spirituality is about religion, but it doesn't have to be. In fact I think most people are Spiritual no matter if they are religious or not! Spirituality is about understanding and exploring your higher purpose, your interconnectedness to all of creation, and living authentically. It is my goal to help you feel inspired and fulfilled.

I do this by asking questions, giving suggestions, and then helping develop ways of marking progress and providing accountability. You don't have to believe the same way I, or anyone else, does. The coaching is centered around your needs and beliefs. I can't do the work for you, but I can help you with motivation and seeing things from a new perspective. Contact me now to schedule a free 15 minute initial consultation.

Understanding Soul Contracts

Soul contracts sound ominous and risky. They bring to mind images of Faust and Pictures of Dorian Grey. Books and plays have been written about them and tales and rumours abound about what they are. It's fun to think in terms of television magic and immortality and becoming omnipotent all through a simple negotiation and signing on the bottom line, fine print and all, but soul contracts actually have nothing to do with the wonderful world of filmation. Now don't get me wrong, I'm not suggesting that those kind of soul contracts don't exist, rather I am talking about a different kind of soul contract, the kind the universe brings to your door at the moment of your existence.

Let me start at the beginning, the kind of soul contract (and yes, that is the correct term) that I am talking about is your fate or destiny according to the universe. To quote Shakespeare, "a rose by any other name would smell as sweet" is completely a misnomer. Your name in reality is the simplified "terms" of your soul contract. If your life is a book, your soul contract as defined by your name is the Coles' Notes version. When we are born, most of us are given a name by our parents or some other respected authority. In many cultures or religions, this name choosing is considered a great privilege. But is the name we receive really just luck or chance? I don't know how many times I've heard other parents in the mall yelling out their child's name and it always seems to be the same three names. The name you were given can actually define your character, personality, talents, and even give you a heads up about major life events or shapers that you will encounter. No, I'm not saying your name can predict your future.

But in reading a soul contract for a client, I can see the events or influencers that their life has or may encounter.

How do you read a soul contract? I'm only going to say that through a series of mathematical computations, the underlying story is readable. It's like a word problem in algebra though more that a basic BEDMAS equation. The one right answer can be manipulated to show you different aspects such as problem-solving strengths, life events, talents, character, even where your hidden threats may come from. Calculating a soul contract is very much like the study of numerology. Your birthdate and time however cannot be altered. Your name can.

What do I mean? The name you are given at birth does show all these details of your life. But that name is not the be all and end all. In many cultures, when the child seems to suffer an "unlucky" life, that family may go to visit the wise person, a shaman, or a psychic to help them alter the "luck". They choose another name at the suggestion of someone who understands how the letters and numbers change our path. Even in North America, the changing of one's name is fairly common. Not just in the changing of your last name to that of your partner. On occasion, the name is changed for work, or for ease, or for impulse. The changed name will change and influence your story/your fate. Nicknames, pet names, gender change names. All of these speak volumes as to who you are over and above how they make you sound. So next time you are trying to decide what to call your child, your pet, yourself, see if you can get some help and a heads up for what's to come.

—*Dana Lee Beaudreau*

Death Rituals Around The World

In Canada, we are really only familiar with two different kinds of funeral: the traditional burial, and the cremation, but there are hundreds of funeral rites and rituals across the world. Each culture has their own traditions that reflect the cultures and religions they come from and reflect how said culture deals with grief. Here are a small selection of lesser known death rituals for Samhain / Halloween.

Sky Burials (bya gtor)

Sky burials are a Tibetan practice specifically among Buddhists. They believe in sending their soul towards heaven, and the Tibetan name, bya gtor means "bird-scattered". It is practiced in Chinese provinces and autonomous regions of Tibet, Qinghai, Sichuan and Inner Mongolia, and Mongolia, Bhutan and parts of India like Sikkim and Zanskar. A body is placed on a sacred place called the charnel grounds. Charnel grounds are sacred sites that are elevated and are for the decomposition or putrefaction of human remains.

The body would be left at the charnel grounds uncovered for wildlife (usually birds) to eat it as it decays. For Tibetan Buddhists, sky burials and cremations were important and showed the impermanence of life. Sky burial in particular was seen as a act of generosity as it fed the animals around the charnel grounds and gave back to nature. Unlike western cultures, they feel no need to preserve the body, as once the soul is gone, it's only an empty vessel.

Unfortunately due to religious marginalization, urbanization, and it being considered a relic of "the old cultures" within China, and the closure of many charnal grounds, it's popularity has waned but it is still practiced in the more remote regions.

Famadihana (the turning of the bones)

A funeral tradition from the native Malagasy people of Madagascar. The turning of the bones is a more recent tradition likely originating around the 17th century. It is likely influenced by southern Asian traditions that believe the soul can only move on after full decomposition. 7 years after the death and burial, the family comes together and exhumes the body and rewraps it in new silks. They proceed to dance to live music while holding the body over their heads. They dance around the tomb before returning it to the family crypt. This is a celebration of the life the person had, rather than a tearful event and was known to reunite families even if there is tension between them.

Famadihana is beginning to decline in popularity due to how expensive it is to buy the silks required to do the ritual. The practice was also decried by missionaries and the church who were trying to stomp out the practice as they colonize- I mean "convert" the native peoples. The Catholic church in modern times claims to no longer have a problem with the practice because it is "cultural, not religious." as if the two can be separated. The practice was linked to the transmission of the pneumonic plague and the Malagasy government put in restrictions on the ritual upon those who have died of the plague, which may have aided to the decline in the practice.

Korean Death Beads

South Korea is a very densely populated area and because of that, cremation was the most logical solution to burial. As the population grows the traditional cremation-

-urns and family crypts also have become a space issue as well so they came up with a new tradition: death beads.

They take the cremains of the deceased and make them into tiny luminescent beads that are kept in glass jars and bowls in the house. This is a newer tradition that costs around $900 to do. The death beads have drawn some criticism with critics saying that it is essentially a soulless cash grab, but worse things were said about cremation in the west when it was introduced.

Funeral Strippers

In Taiwan and some parts of China, it was common to have funeral strippers. They were a sign of wealth and social status. Business men, government officials, and important social figures were known to have them. There were spiritual significance of course. Having the strippers was said to "appease wandering spirits" and give one last hurrah to the departed. They would dance and strip on non lit stages but with music, and DJ's, though they rarely undressed completely.

In Chinese and Taiwanese tradition, the more people that showed up to a funeral, the better one's trip to the afterlife would be. The funeral strippers served a dual purpose as a display of social status, and as a tactic to draw people in to the funeral processions. The Chinese government disapproves of the practice, and is trying to end it but it survives in rural areas.

Personally, I wouldn't mind strippers at my own funeral, but I doubt that's allowed in Canada.

Natural Burials

A return to basic traditions after the standardization of embalming in the west. Natural burials are exactly what they sound like. You wrap the body in a shroud that will -

-decompose with the body. You place the body in a biodegradable coffin, and bury them in a shallow grave to allow for natural decomposition without the pollution of the water table associated with an embalmed corpse.

You can have home viewings with natural burials or a traditional viewing depending on the laws in your province, territory, or state. Despite what the funeral industry will tell you, they were never illegal. As long as you can follow local laws around the handling of a corpse as well as find a funeral house that will work with you, natural burials are a cheaper and more green alternative to traditional funerals.

-Desirée Goulden

Grief & Cookies

It's been almost a year since I've lost my great grandmother, the woman who was my rock. I thought by now that I would know what to say, how to process it, something more clever to say than, I still want to scream, it's not fair and I miss her. Is it bad enough that I have the object permanence of a goldfish, so I forget that she's gone. So it's been almost a year of it hitting me, over and over again like it was the first time. That's something that's not talked about enough when it comes to grieving.

Someone at my church, which was my nanna's church, asked me what she was like. And I blanked, so I mentioned her baking and her divinity. Yes, she was known for her divinity at the church bake sales, but she was so much more than that. Yes, she spent a lot of time in that church, but she was more than that church. She was a mother, a grandmother, and eventually great grandmother to 3. She was a wife. She loved to garden. I could talk about how she was president of the garden club and was well known for her roses. There was always coffee on the pot for guest and always cookies..

I could talk about the fact that she grew up in the great depression as the honorary boy for her dad after he lost his arm in a tractor accident. I could tell stories she doesn't know I know about her sneaking out and drinking, and probably on a few nights, almost dying behind a barn.

I wish I could tell you her pigs name. I long forgot that before I could even think to ask her.

Yet, it all feels shallow, because I can remember these things, but it still doesn't feel right. Because, yes, absolutely for a moment she can live on in stories, but I still can't hug her. I can't sit down and watch Lawrence Welk with her. She'll never curl my hair again, even though it never needed the curler. I can't go to a movie with her just for her to nap through it, she always said she had some of the best naps then.

I also kicked myself, because I had so much time I could have asked her and written everything down. But, when you're young, you don't realize how real that loss will be when it happens. You think, "Oh, I want to remember, they're good memories, of course I'll always have them." But, no, if there's one fact about anything I've learned is, you can't always rely on your memories.

I watched my nanna start to lose hers due to dementia, and I still didn't think to ask her to write them down. I watched her slip away from us all while she was still here, but I can't change the past. I can only start to write down the memories I have and the lessons she taught me while I still have them in my head.

So, maybe I can't hug her again, but I still remember the smell of peanut butter cookies made on the spot because the guests wanted cookies. She assured them all, it was no big deal. And it wasn't, it's simply:

1 egg, 1 cup of sugar, and 1 cup of peanut butter. Bake at 350 for 7-10 minutes. And maybe the grief isn't such a big deal either, maybe I can deal with it like she made cookies, as she needed them. I long forgot that before I could even think to ask her.

—Owen Lee Heavenhill

The Misconceptions About Ouija Boards

Ouija boards are dangerous.

This is what we are told constantly. Not only from Christians, but from people within the pagan and witchy spheres as well. We are taught that they are inherently dangerous and you need to be a very experienced witch to use them, and you need to use a lot of protection while using them. They can usher in demons, trickster spirits, and can get you possessed.

It is actually rather comical to hear these same comments come from both sides. Especially considering that they're talking about a children's board game that was created for and sold at Walmart.

Let's talk for a moment about the origins of the Ouija board because there seems to be a lot of misinformation circulating about them.

The Ouija board is also known as the spirit board or the talking board and was created on July 1st 1980 by Elijah Bond. It was originally intended to be a normal board game but unfortunately it was created during the Victorian spiritualist movement. The spiritualist movement was a occult movement in the 1900's that consisted of the idea that anyone could communicate with the dead and spirits through crystal gazing and other forms of divination. One might say that the spiritualist movement helped pave the way for modern occult practices. There may have been many ligament mediums, psychics, and people with clairsenses within the spiritualist movement, there were also way more frauds. The frauds were usually the ones that got all the media attention. You may recall the Cottingley Fairies photographs taken by the spiritualist's Elsie Wright and Frances Griffiths, which would go on to spread en mass a of misinformation and culturally appropriative narratives about the fae.

One of these spiritualists was Pearl Curran, who brought fame to the Ouija board by allegedly contacting the dead. "Many moons ago I lived. Again, I come. Patience Worth, my name." was the first message she got through the board, and over the months Pearl would build an entire narrative and character around "Patience". By 1915 Pearl and Patience were having sessions where Patience would give her from 500 to 3000 words in a single sitting. This is... Ridiculous and as a medium myself, I can say with absolute certainty that it was nothing more that Pearl being an excellent saleswoman and con-artist.

None the less, the Ouija board would go on to gain fame and infamy in the occult world and beyond. In recent years the dramatic and over the top travel channel show, Ghost Adventures, had an entire episode based around a Ouija board demon named Zozo. Apparently this is a demon of destruction that is summoned through the Ouija board and can possess people and has followed people through generations and... the story can be tracked back to a bare bones 2000s website called "true ghost tales". People claim that Zozo is no less than 3 different entities, all of which are tricksters and most of them have "African" heritage, dispite the closet mention of the entity being from a 1818 French book called Le Dictionnaire Infernal.

If you are starting to see a trend here, you're not alone. It seems the majority of scary stories surrounding the Ouija board are all from less than reputable sources likely looking for media attention. Now I am not saying that spirit communication is not possible, but I am saying that you are not going to get possessed and have your house haunted because you bought a Ouija board from Walmart. (Which you can do by the way. It was $20 last time I checked.)

Ouija boards can be used for divination just like tarot, automatic writing, pendulums, and the like. Some may indeed use them to contact the dead, but the danger of doing that is only the same danger that is associated with anyone who preforms necromancy. Necromancy is any magic or practice that is related to contacting the dead. From ancestor work to speaking to lost family, necromancy is more common than people seem to think. Depending on what you're doing with the dead, you're going to deal with a certain amount of danger. There is a reason why more advanced practitioners get frustrated when we see younger practitioners saying that they are doing automatic writing with their deity or ancestor. Any form of divination that involves any spirit physically manipulating your body, like the Ouija board does, is dangerous and can open you up to possession.

The thing is; when practitioners do these things, we know what we're doing. We know how to invite spirits in, and banish them after. We know how to protect ourselves against possession and we know how to handle these things if they do happen. We know and accept the risks associated with necromancy and low tier possession and physical manipulation. We go in to these settings with the tools to handle them.

The problem is as always, the non occult practitioner "spooky people" who get their shits and giggles from messing with the dead.

These people don't seem to realize that there is a danger to these things inherently. The will use the Spirit Box communication method constantly, get just as haunted and because they looked at a Ouija board once, they'll blame the Ouija board. Obviously you are going to get harassed and haunted if you constantly antagonize and bother the dead, and it is silly to blame the Ouija board rather than accepting that this is the result of your own actions.

Ouija boards are not dangerous. Necromancy is. Necromancy is the act of contacting the dead. If you do not know how to safely do that, don't do it. If you do... don't blame the Ouija board.

-Desirée Goulden

Candles

What's more witchy than a good candle? Here are a selection of TalesOfTheGods approved candles for you to buy the next time you're looking for one!

The original creator of the crystal pyramid candles is back at it with her new business and pyramids!

Made with quality wax and scents and with over 65 hours of burn time, these candles are a must have. Each candle has crystals inside waiting for you as you burn the candle down making it a wonderful gift!

https://selaluzcandles.com

Need a spell? Look no further than ThugBrujo from TikTok! His spell candles are amazingly effective and aesthetically pleasing to boot! Hand carved and worth every penny!

https://www.candlelitglow.com

Need candles for your altar or for your own spells? Grove and Grotto as usual, has your back. Pick up a 20 pack of multi coloured chime candles and whatever else you may need!

https://www.groveandgrotto.com

Do you have a product or service you offer? Are you looking for free advertisement? Contact us at TalesOTheGods@gmail.com and we will run your add in the next edition of the TalesOfTheGods & Practical Witchcraft magazine!

Grief

  Griefs talked about a lot, I feel like I've talked about it a lot. But, it's also not talked about enough. There's a weird catch 22, where it's talked about, but from a neurotypical, usually christian stand point. Grief looks different for everybody though and so let me share a couple of lessons I've learned in the almost year since my great grandmother has passed.

  The first lesson being, object permanence can absolutely effect the grieving process. For me personally, I either completely forgot about her existence for a moment, which is heartbreaking, or I'll forget that she's passed and I can't call her. They both have their issues, and they both feel like they cause hurdles in whatever the grieving process is supposed to be.

  Number two, I don't think there really is a specific process. We can try and lay out a roadmp and say you may deal with grief, denail, anger, etc, but I've seen some people completely accept the death and seem to never go through any of that. It all depends on so much, and not to sound crude, but having already started grieving them for whatever reason in their life, doesn't make a difference. It just, extends your grieving process.

  Not everyone will grieve. Some people, literally do just accept that they're dead and move on. I thought that was going to be me, seeing as I knew I would still be able to contact her and death is an inevitabltly. And yes, while I did fully accept her death even before she'd actually passed, what hurt me was not being able to call her up and ask her for advice on cooking, household things. It was the little things. Yes, in all seriousness, I could use my mediumship abilities to try and ask her still, and believe me, I have, but it's not the same.

While most spirits and most of your ancestors will still have some of their human memories, they will lose some of them immediately upon passing. They'll remember some of the most basic mundane things, like their microwave chocolate fudge recipe, but if you want to ask them what the name of their pig was growing up, it's crickets.

Some people have said that grief comes in waves, but maybe this is also tied to my object permanence causing issues, mine likes to hit me like a deer flying across the interstate with not a care in the world. I don't like the wave analogy because that implies that you can see it coming. And, yes, that might ring true for some, but others may have different analogies. I think, it doesn't matter what analogy you're going to use, just make sure you use one that feels right to the way it works for you. If you ever have to describe your grief and how it effects you, it needs to be an accurate analogy.

Some days the analogies don't fit and I just want to burn everything down because all I need. Is to hear her voice one more time and just sit and have dinner with her. But I can't, either one, so instead on those days, I'll scream, cry, throw a pillow if I need, drink coffee, maybe a glass of wine to her, and maybe do something in honor of her, usually cleaning something if I'm going to be honest. Are there days where all it does is make the whole feel bigger? Yes. And on those days, I give mysef the grace to wallow in memories if I need to.

The biggest thing I've learned about grief though, is sometimes its a month by month basis, sometimes its week to week, and sometimes its second to second. It's been almost a year, and I won't say I feel like I've gotten through it. I will say that I've better learned how to live with it. And if I never make it past that point, that's a fine point to have made it to.

-Owen Lee Heavenhill

For This I am Ever Thankful

I am writing this even though the idea is fairly commonplace. How do we show gratitude to our guides, gods, and goddesses? I know that we all have our own way of acknowledging the help we receive in performing our craft. For some of us we glean help from our ancestors, or spirit guides. For others of us we receive our help from our god(s) or goddess(es). For others of us the help comes from the fairy realm or the Others. But I know that even in my case, it can be really easy to forget to say thank you.

At this time of year, I feel like we/I should take some time to re-evaluate my own habits and place some new ones into my routine to show the gratitude that I own to the one who guides me. As a Christian witch, I do lean most on God. But as an Ojibwe descendant, I also have called upon my spirit guides or ancestors to assist on occasion. So, to be clear, I am not telling you who you need to be aligned with, I'm merely opening up a discussion. gratitude. And I'd welcome anyone else out there to share with me what their routine, ceremony, or habits are in showing thanks to their guides or helpers.

Gratitude for me involves both ceremony and habits. I do make offerings of blessed or moon water to the earth on a full moon or a special occasion and on occasion I may even offer a toast of wine or spirits. I try to keep a gratitude journal, where I record three things that have been a joy or a blessing (even if it is small or insignificant) that happened that day and say a word of thanks before sleep. I light my candles in ceremony before I kneel in prayer in the new moon.

My routine? (order in which I light my candles – yes colour is involved)

First set: Earth, Air, Fire Water Spirit - red

Second set: sun, moon, stars - blue

Third set: North, south, east, west - green

Fourth set: Father, Son, Holy ghost. - white

Final candle: Amen - white

I know that meant nothing to most of you. It wasn't meant to. Ceremony is very personal. Each and every person has their own way and their own call to heart. Each person has their own ritual and strength. I want to invite you all to take a moment and think about what yours is and know that gratitude, that thankful heart that you are sharing with your guide, in my mind strengthens the positive energy that feeds the Earth and the Universe. Let's keep the power growing.

—Dana Lee Beaudreau

What Is A Death Witch?

There are many closed and secretive practices within paganism, the religions, paths, and the occult. One of these paths is the path of the Death Witch, but what is that?

Death Witch may be both a singular path, or an umbrella term for many similar paths that are oriented around the ushering of souls across the veil. Death Witchery is a very secretive path that can be handed down through families and traditions and what one Death Witch does may be completely different than what another does. What is common however are a few things:

1) They usher the souls of the dead across to their respective afterlife, whether they are a soul that's trapped or whether they are hired to help someone across the moment they pass.

2) The work they do is dangerous to themselves, and has physical repercussions making it a very specialized skill set that is not a path for most people.

3) They need to have a mentor, and the initiation process is dangerous and mandatory for the Death Witch in question to complete to earn their title.

I myself am a subsect of Death Witch known as a Psychopomp. I have been in training for just over a year, and would still consider to be new as the training for a Death Witch can be as long as 10 years.

Many won't talk about their paths due to the darker nature of it and how personal it is, but I don't mind dipping into some of my own practice, which more or less the same as many others who claim to be Psychopomps. Please note, that while we fall under the umbrella term of "Death Witch" it does follow a Hellenic Pagan path and other paths may conflict or be different to my own.

I started my path via a justice working. I was doing a working to sway a court case in 2020 and had to pay a price for their aid: use my mediumship skills to become a messenger for the gods and humans, and to help Hermes in the moving of souls as a Psychopomp. This was long before I had even herd of Death Witches.

That night was the first night I did any sort of Psychopompary. He lead me via the the astral to several of the dead and I got the first glimpse of what would be expected of me and why it was important. I was brought to a old man who died alone in his study with nobody close to notice his passing. I was brought to a house where a child committed suicide as his parents found him. Hermes ended up dealing with that spirit personally due to its aggression and emotional distress. I was brought to many lost and hurt souls that night in order to test to see what I was personally able to handle emotionally.

I would come to understand a few things as I continued on my training with him. (I am still in training, and likely will be for years) The first of which was that Psychopomp entities, deities, and spirits from many pantheons and beliefs help other religions and paths in regards to helping the dead to were they ought to be. Because of that, I would have to learn of and accept many path's beliefs and deities, even those (Christianity) that I have personally been harmed by or disagree with. The second was that no matter how many Psychopomps there are in the world, there are always going to be outnumbered by millions of dead souls due to the population of the earth. This is one of the many reasons why we have lost and wandering souls.

The third is that in most cases where I personally am involved, it will be to guide souls who have died in terrible ways and are in major emotional distress.

There are a few souls that just need some guidance, but they are always going to be outnumbered by the distressed ones. People need Psychopomps and Death Witches in order to to help move these souls that can not be handled by the common folk. There is always a physical toll to this. Some people have body aches, I personally become mentally drained and tired but am unable to make my body sleep for days. Dealing this personally with the dead and the magical energy needed to move them will draw from you just as normal magical workings do. Unlike magical workings, however, these can last hours and drain you very fast. There is a notion going around that Death Witches don't live long lives due to this, but I personally live off of spite so I don't plan on dying before 97 no matter how tired I am. (I can practically hear the Fates laughing at me)

Psychopompary is a very interesting practice, and a very needed one. I have only met one other Psychopomp aside from myself. They were also put on this path and trained by Hermes. I can't tell people to get into it or seek it out, as it takes someone who is able to see the worst of the worse and still hold themselves together. If you are meant for this path a teacher will reach out to you for your respective path, whether it be a deity or other initiated practitioner.

If you have been contacted about starting on that path I urge you to consider it. If you want to help the dead and dying without being a Death Witch, look into death positivity. There is a lot of jobs in death work and the death positivity movement is a growing one that always needs more people. End of life care may be working as a mortician, death doula, end of life councillor and planning, grief counseling, and more. You can visit your local graveyard and tend to and clean the graves, set up altars for your lost loved ones, and educate yourself on local and foreign death rituals.

If you know any kind of Death Witch, ask them about their practice if they are okay with sharing. We are a secretive and often misunderstood bunch that can seem scary by the name alone. Our job is to help, and we don't bite.

Unless you ask.

—Desirée Goulden

The Future, Regrettably
Coming soon!

The debut urban fantasy novel from Desirée Goulden, prequel to the Aurora Garroway series.

Julian is a man with nothing but a name. Woken from a coma and thrust into a war he does not want to fight, he is the body guard and right hand man of a tyrannical cult leader, Rose. Escape is futile and attempts cause innocent people to be killed to keep him in line. With death as the only escape, he becomes reckless in battle, hoping to be cut down and finally escape the life he is trapped in.

Rose notices and offers him a boon: stay in line and do as she says and he will be able to visit the future in his dreams. He will be able to live a comfortable life and see why the Conduit Hierarchy's war is just, and how it will better the world.

Will this be enough to pacify Julian? Or will this motivate him to tear down the organization that seeks to control him, and find the truth?

(Crystals)

Crystals have become a mainstay in new age practice. Crystals contain and can help move and transform energy that we can use in out practice and lives. While many more traditional paths do not often involve crystals, and certainly not in the way new age practitioners use them, they are very common in many paths now-a-days

(Agate)
Prosperity, health, abundance, ward against negativity

(Amber)
Purification, ease of pain, ward against negativity, grieving, protection, illness recovery, beauty, fertility

(Amethyst)
Royalty, intuition, sobriety, peace, calm, creativity

(Bloodstone)
Renewal, presentness, self-confidence, victory over enemies, breaking down of others defenses, unselfishness, intuition

(Clear quartz)
Clarity, focus, cleansing, healing, purify energy, calmness, inner peace

(Hematite)
Grounding, money, decisions, manifestations, money, focus, stability, balance, divination, problem solving, communication, strength

(Jade)
Clarity, focus, cleansing, healing, purify energy, calmness, inner peace

(Jasper)
Grounding, money, decisions, manifestations, money, focus, stability, balance, divination, problem solving, communication, strength

Crystals

Lapis Lazuli
Opens minds, self awareness, self esteem, peace, harmony, morality

Moonstone
Connecting to feminine energy, fertility, calming, the moon, intuition, remove negativity, protection when travelling at night, balance

Obsidian
Scrying, protection, ward against negativity, blocks psychic attacks, clarity, past life healing

Opal
Love, passion, desire, freedom, independence, realizing potential, creativity, good luck

Rose quartz
Strengthening love, sex, passion, blocks nightmares, calms conflict, emotional healing

Selenite
The moon, protection, cleansing, purity, innocence, spiritual growth

Tiger's Eye
Fearlessness, certainty, courage, grace, action, wisdom, understanding beyond emotional interference

Turquoise
Dream work, fertility, wards against negativity, happiness, compassion, manifestation, creativity, clear communication, intuition

(Plant & herbs)

(Apple)

Love, healing, fertility, immortality, beauty. The wood is prime for wand making.

(Basil)
Happiness, peace, love, money attraction, protection.

(Black Pepper)

Protection, healing.

(Chamomile)

Money, peace, love, tranquility, purification, aids in meditation.

(Cinnamon)

Love, happiness, money.

(Clove)

Luck, prosperity, friendship, stops gossip.

(Garlic)

Repel unwanted advances, used in love magic, used in baneful workings, repels the evil eye and thieves, luck, love, aphrodisiac, exorcisms, strength, spell breaking.

(Lavender)

Purification, clarity, fertility, love

(Lemon)

Purification, cleansing, love, repel or break spells against you, turns away the evil eye.

(Oregano)

Happiness, joy tranquility, luck, health, protection, letting go, strengthen love.

(Plant & herbs)

(Parsley)
Necromancy, strength, passion, vitality, sobriety.

(Rosemary)
Fidelity, the removal of jealousy, memory, recollection of dreams, money, cleansing of negativity.

(Sage (Not white))
Cleansing, immortality, protection, grant wishes, wisdom, easing pain from the death of a loved one.

(Star Anise)
Youth, repel nightmares, lust, blessings, exorcisms, aids divination, attracts spirits.

(Thyme)
Strength, courage, positivity, remove negativity, remove sadness, happy dreams, repel nightmares.

pagans & cremation.

In 2014 47% of people within the USA chose cremation over traditional burial, but how many people know that without Pagans, you would most likely not be able to have that option?

While cremation was always around in some form (There are records of burning bodies as funeral processes as far back as Ancient Athens ((1100 BC))) across the world, American Christian grievers were taken aback at the thought of them. American at the time of the first cremation (1876) were very concerned with the preservation of one's self after death and referred to cremation as dehumanizing and disgusting. Caitlin Doughty, Mortician, owner of Clarity Funerals and Cremation of Los Angeles, author, and YouTuber, reports that one of the reviewers of the first cremation called it "Another exemplification of the wickedness of the metropolis" which should give you an idea as to how the general populous thought of cremation.

Cremation wouldn't really shake its stigma and become popular until the 1980's, but if it wasn't for the Theosophical Society Of America, I have my doubts that it ever would be as popular as what it is now. But what is the Theosophical Society and what happened during the first cremation?

The Theosophical Society Of America was formed in 1875 by Helena Petrovna Blavatsky, noblewoman, Colonel Henry Steel Olcott and William Quan Judge, attorneys and 16 others.

This religious movement hand amongst its members noblemen and women and influential people of status, including Thomas Edison and William Butler Yeats.

The Society states its beliefs as follows from it's website, https://www.theosophical.org/ "Ever since its founding in 1875, the Theosophical Society has stood for freedom of thought and respect for all people regardless of race, class, caste, sex, or religion. To join the Theosophical Society, you are required to have no specific beliefs. You need only to state your agreement with the Society's Three Objects:

1. To form a nucleus of the universal brotherhood of humanity, without distinction of race, creed, sex, caste, or color.

2. To encourage the comparative study of religion, philosophy, and science.

3. To investigate unexplained laws of nature and the powers latent in humanity."
It draws it's belief system from Vedānta, Mahāyāna Buddhism, Qabbalah, and Sufism and wants to unite Eastern and Western practices to show the commonality of human culture.

Given this rather progressive thinking (particularly for the 1870's) it is easy to see how this group would straddle the line of what was acceptable and what was obscene for the time. It seems people could not come to a conclusion as to what to think of the group as they either loved or hated the idea. None the less, regardless of the public opinion, they made it a goal to push forward with presenting cremation to the western world. A move allowed only by their titles, and class, and money, no doubt.

The first cremation was the cremation of Baron Joseph Henry Louis Charles, Baron de Palm, who died after battling with an illness that effected many of his organs.

He left his body and much of his estate to Olcott for his kindness to him in life. He also requested in his will that no clergyman or priest should officiate at his funeral.

His funeral was held as the Masonic Temple in New York on the corner of 23rd Street and 6th Avenue on May 20, 1876. His funeral was a grand spectacle that many "reviewers" showed up to report upon for local news papers. There was roughly 2000 guests for the Baron's funeral. It was due to this media presence that we know what happened during the funerary ceremonies. One of re reporters from The New York Times called the ceremony "a hodge-podge of notions, a mixture of guess-work and jugglery, of elixirs and pentagons, of charms and conjurations"

The ceremonies consisted of "a home-brewed liturgy of Hindu scriptures, passages from Charles Darwin's writings, scraps of spiritualism and transcendentalism, references to fire worship, and invocations of the Nile goddess Isis" and were called "Folly," "farce," "weird," "objectionable," "repulsive," "revolting," "a desecration" "one might have supposed that the company had been assembled to have a good time over roast pig." (via https://www.questia.com/) To the common Christen citizen of the day, this may very well have seemed to be a barbaric display of glee over the death of the Baron. To modern practitioners, this may seem to be a appropriation of many cultures and religions with no real acknowledgement of the fact that if anyone of the cultures of which the Theosophical Society took from tried this, the already abysmal reception would have been far worse.

So they had their ceremony and weather they had wanted the negative press or not, they caught the attention of the United States Of America. Did this allow for them to cremate the body? No. In fact it would be 6 months before the Baron could be cremated. Dr. Francis Julius LeMoyne designed the crematorium that would eventually cremate De Palm.

LeMoyne had the plans for his crematorium for some time, as he began to worry about pollution from the decomposing bodies after traditional burial (a thought process that at the time were unfounded but if he lived today with the commonplace of embalming would have been a valid concern) but was bound by his own money for the project and hindered by protests every step of the way. All while De Palm waited for his body to be tended to. You can't really blame people at the time for disliking the process. I imagine that this would be extremely macabre to the common folk, especially when you consider that they lost the body of De Palm amongst the cargo on the train carrying him to the crematory. You can't blame them from being struck with fear when he was put into the machine finally and his arm stuck up and apparently raising 3 fingers (it is a normal part of the crematory process for the limbs to curl up and contort as the body burns and the liquid vaporizes out of the body).

Despite the spectacle and outrage, the LeMoyne crematory would continue to cremate bodies after that. It closed in 1901 after cremating 42 bodies, LeMoyne included. His ashes were buried on the property and a headstone stands over them to this day.

As for De Palm, his remains were put into a "Hindu-style urn" and spectators took with them some of his ashes. LeMoyne took some of his bones to keep on his desk and there were rumours that some of the Theosophical Society kept some of De Palm's ashes in snuff boxes which they carried on them, although that may have just been a fanciful rumour.

Since then, cremations became more and more common until today where they account for around half of funerals in America. We may never know if cremation would have become acceptable if it weren't for LeMoyne, De Palm and The Theosophical Society, I for one doubt it would have, but none the less we have them to thank for cremation.

I can't help but to think that one could make a interesting historical comedy based off these events. If you want to know more, head to AskAMortician on YouTube, or watch the connected video beneath this.

It's always interesting to see where Pagan influence lies in modern society, and this shows that we can all make positive change in the world. Even if you're a penniless faux Baron, a strange old man with dreams of burning corpses, or a person who thinks cremation is the only way to stop vampires (listen it was the 1800's it was a valid concern back in the day) never doubt that you as a Pagan can bring about change.

-Desirée Goulden

Tales Of The Gods

Free shops & services listings

Have a shop or service and want to extend your reach without speding some coin? Contact us! We will set up your shop in our public database including a explination of your business and a landing page to display your wares!

We will post you on our online shops and services for free! Just contact us at our contact page on TalesOfTheGods.com or send us a email at TalesOTheGods@gmail.com or at our social medias! We can be found on Facebook, Twitter, and Instagram!

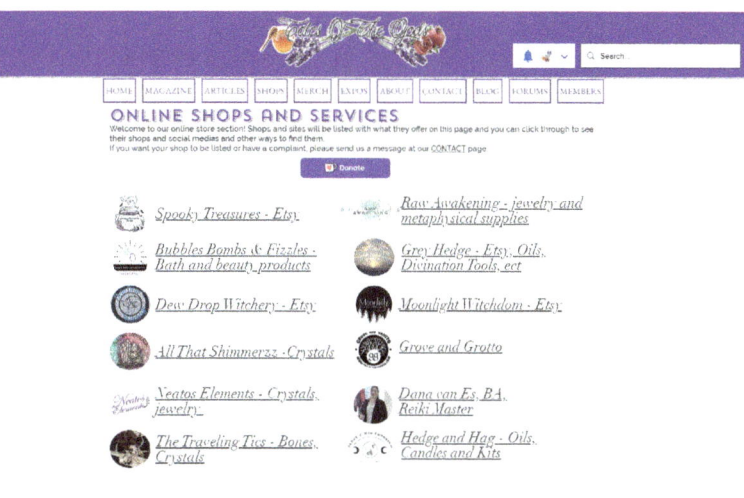

Magazine Updates

The Yule edition marks the one year anniversary of the TalesOfTheGods & Practical Witchcraft magazine! Since the beginning this magazine has gone through many changes. Staff changes, publisher changes, format changes, and more! Not all of these changes have come without growing pains.

You may have noticed the last 3 editions were not released on the day of the wheel of the year for which they are named. Recently we have changed to a new publisher, IngramSpark. As IngramSpark distributes to hundreds of book stores across the world both online and off, it takes time for sellers to get the copies of the magazine. On top of this, there is also a fee of about $60 cad that has to be paid to publish the magazine. As this is a small group of creators, and is made with a budget of $0, that money comes out of pocket on my end and thus if a publication date falls in the middle of the month I may not be able to pay said fee.

We are working on changing this but it takes time as it requires shifting the entire production time back a month. The Yule edition will come out on time, and likely earlier as we finally hit a part of the wheel of the year where we aren't essentially publishing month after month back to back.

We also have finally figured out the problems regarding the digital editions, and from now on out there should be no problem with the Kindle print reproduction of the magazine.

People have been contacting us about creating a subscription for the magazine, and we are working on it. It is likely that a digital edition subscription will be implemented but it is a work in process and will likely result in PDF's being distributed rather than Kindle editions. Like I said, this is a work in process and the details are being ironed out. A physical subscription will be created in time, but that will most likely be done in mid to late 2022.

We decided to axe the TalesOfTheGods & Practical Witchcraft Archives due to a lack of interest, and settled on a once yearly collection of all the magazines in that said year. After Yule you will be able to find the 2021 compilation which will be a single hardback book containing the full colour editions of all the magazines within it. It will also contain contributor bios and information about the magazine. You will be able to see the improvements over the year, and the journey from a small KDP publication to a more professional and constant witchy magazine.

We thank you for your patience and for sticking with us through our journey. We look forward to the coming years, and to bringing you pagan and occult entertainment, education, and news for people of all paths and levels of experience.

www.ingramcontent.com/pod-product-compliance
Lightning Source LLC
Chambersburg PA
CBHW042018090526
44589CB00023B/2836